Great Smoky Mountains
SIMPLY BEAUTIFUL

Photography by Adam Jones

Text by Steve Kemp

FARCOUNTRY

COVER:
Autumn paints the sprawling hardwood forests of
the Great Smoky Mountains in bold reds and golds.

BACK COVER:
The Little Pigeon River flows clear as glass through
the Greenbrier area of the national park.

FRONT FLAP:
The Carter Shields cabin resides along the Cades
Cove Loop Road.

TITLE PAGE:
A summer sunrise viewed from Clingmans Dome
reveals the weathered silhouettes of the ancient
Great Smoky Mountains.

COPYRIGHT PAGE:
The waters of the Little Pigeon River are home
to rainbow and brook trout.

ISBN 1-56037-304-0

© 2004 Farcountry Press

Photographs © Adam Jones

FOREWORD BY STEVE KEMP

Local people, those from families like Ogle, Huskey, Palmer, Lawson, Caldwell, and Walker, families whose roots in the area go back eight generations or more, are extremely proud of their Great Smoky Mountains. Most have been around the country some, been to Colorado and California, and have come back with renewed conviction that the Great Smokies are the most beautiful mountains in the world.

To be frank, many locals aren't overly impressed at the sight of mountains without trees, of icy peaks and arid foothills where no rhododendron could possibly grow. To locals, mountains are pret-ty because that's where the red bud and mountain laurel bloom, it's where the wood thrush and winter wren sing, it's where a black bear leads her two cubs to a patch of blueberries.

Nature reaches a crescendo in the Great Smoky Mountains of western North Carolina and east Tennessee. Life is luxuriant, abundant, and incredibly diverse. An old-growth yellow birch tree in the rain-drenched Smokies' high country may have an eight-foot-tall red spruce tree growing on one limb and a healthy clump of Catawba rhododendron sprouting from its crook. There may be three species of ferns rooted in its rough bark and a dozen varieties of mosses, lichens, and bryophytes thriving on the north and east sides of its trunk. A family of northern flying squirrels could live in a cavity, and it wouldn't be surprising to find a black snake working its way toward the nest of a Canada warbler. If you shook the tree hard enough, 75 or more species of insects might flutter to the ground.

One of the reasons the Smokies harbor such a treasure trove of life is that nature has been relatively kind to these mountains over the past 175 million years or so. Across this unfathomable span of time, the Smokies, unlike much of North America, have neither been submerged beneath oceans nor frozen and scoured by mile-thick glaciers. Plants and animals have had plenty of time to settle in, to find a niche, to multiply, to allow the poker game of genetics, isolation, and competition to spawn new species.

Not that things have been dull in the southern Appalachians. During the many glacier advances of the Pleistocene epoch, the last of which ended a mere 10,000 years ago, massive ice sheets never reached as far south as the Smokies—but they came pretty close. In what is now Ohio, walls of ice loomed like the Cliffs of Dover. Northerly winds blew frigid air off the endless sea of ice, chilling the climate far to the south.

Because the glaciers advanced very slowly, northern forests were able to survive by seed dispersal. Canadian trees and forests ended up on the coastal plain of South Carolina. Above the Great Smokies' timberline stood wind-swept tundra dotted with perennial snowfields. If the Appalachian Mountain Range had trended east–west rather than north–south (as do the Alps of Europe), the escape routes for northern plants would have been blocked and hundreds of species that are familiar today would likely be extinct.

During the many warm periods that also characterize the Pleistocene, the South became inhospitable to the northern immi-grants. Over thousands of years, their populations inched back northward or perished. But in the Smoky Mountain high country, plants and animals found "islands" with long cold winters, cool summers, and other conditions that suited them well enough. They settled into places like Mt. Le Conte, Charlies Bunion, and Clingmans Dome, where they linger to this day.

Southern species like sweet gum, pawpaw, and the green anole went through a similar period of exile and return. They "win-tered" in the Deep South and Mexico, then reclaimed their old stomping grounds in the valleys and foothills of the Smokies when the climate warmed.

Catawba rhododendron bursts into bloom at the park's middle and high elevations during June.

The geography of the Great Smoky Mountains allows northern and southern species to coexist to an extent that borders on the surreal. A Canadian naturalist, blindfolded and airlifted to a stand of spruce and fir at an elevation of 6,000 feet in the Smokies, would see, hear, and smell little to convince him he'd left his native land. Yet, if he were to follow a trail down the mountainside for three or four hours, he would discover an entirely new environment, one with but a few reminders of home.

To be sure, the Smokies' diversity of life is based on more than altitude and glaciers. The 80 or so inches of precipitation that soaks the high peaks each year allows for a certain amount of extravagance among plants and animals. So does a latitude of 35.6° North, a position that encourages a longish, temperate growing season, at least at the low and mid-elevations. Still another influence is the crumpled, jumbled, time-worn geography of the mountains themselves, a factor that contributes to both abundance and diversity.

Plant ecologists, after years and years of research, have been unable to predict accurately where, say, a type of forest called a "beech gap" will appear. The landscape is too complex, with too many subtle variables, to expel all mystery. Within the slopes, gorges, and hollows are a million nooks and crannies that nurture their own unique assemblies of life. Take, for example, the cold, steep, mossy microclimate at the head of Porters Creek. Though not much over 4,000 feet in elevation, the area is almost perpetually in shadow from the ridge that carries the Appalachian Trail. Thunderstorms have a tendency to linger near the crest of the steep ridge, and the area is tormented by flash floods and debris slides. One day in the 1970s, a park ranger exploring the trail-less area discovered a grove of paper birch trees, a 30-foot-tall species that had gone undiscovered in the Great Smoky Mountains even after more than a century of botanical surveys and scientific exploration.

Grassy balds, a habitat unique to the southern and central Appalachians, are not merely hard to predict, they defy explanation entirely. Called balds because they are mostly treeless and appear smooth or "hairless" from a distance, these high-elevation meadows are covered with thick mountain oat grass and other low-growing species that are rare elsewhere in the region. Farmers have summered their sheep, cows, pigs, and other livestock on the balds in pastoral settings reminiscent of *Heidi* or the *Sound of Music*. While some grassy balds are human-made, others, like Gregory and Parson, were noted in the journals of surveyors and explorers who visited the Smokies before the first settlements of European-Americans.

Theories as to the origins of grassy balds abound. Ice storms, wind storms, Native Americans. Grazing by buffalo, elk, or even woolly mammoths. Fire. Gaps between forest types left open by the warming and cooling of the climate during the last ice age. No one theory has gained widespread acceptance, and different balds may actually have different origins. One thing is for certain, though— there are few finer places to be than Gregory Bald at azalea time or Andrews Bald on a crystal clear October morning when the ridges of soft blue mountains roll on forever.

Tree-lined Hyatt Lane winds through a quiet corner of Cades Cove.

The richness and variety of plant life, the persistence of extremely rare stands of Eastern virgin forest, the presence of bear, deer, songbirds, and other wildlife, the beauty of the boulder-strewn rivers and waterfalls—these all are reasons the Great Smoky Mountains were preserved as a national park. Though interest in protecting the Smokies as a park goes back to the nineteenth century, the movement didn't pick up much steam until 1923 when Knoxvillian Anne Davis returned from a vacation out West and asked, "Why can't we have a national park in the Great Smokies?"

Easier said than done; the years between Mrs. Davis's question and the establishment of the national park in 1934 were difficult, even agonizing ones. Unlike the big Western parks such as Yellowstone and Grand Canyon, Great Smoky Mountains National Park could not be created simply by drawing lines on a map of largely uninhabited, government-owned land. More than

5,000 people lived on the land that would become our largest eastern national park. The Reagans, Ogles, Huskeys, Whaleys, and Messers had already lived in the mountains for 75 years or more. They owned two-story whitewashed houses, barns, country stores, fruit orchards, vineyards, sawmills, grist mills, and much more. When the first rumors began circulating that the government was going to buy their land and move them from their homes, the reaction for many was shock and disbelief. "We've worked mighty hard clearing up these old mountains to grow corn. You keep talking about a park. You mean you're gonna turn our land back to them varmints?" was one farm woman's response.

Granted, not everyone was prospering in the mountains. High in the hollers and up the rocky slopes many farmers had already exhausted their marginal land and hunted out most of the game. There was the Depression going on. A good many families were relieved that someone wanted to pay cash for their eroded farms and buy them a chance for a fresh start down the road. Today there are millionaires whose parents or grandparents rode down out of the mountains wearing patched overalls and dresses made from flour sacks and used their buyout money to purchase a few acres of land in what would become the tourist meccas of Gatlinburg and Pigeon Forge.

Proponents of the national park idea also had to settle with the big timber companies who in fact owned the vast majority of the Great Smoky Mountains. They had purchased their land for a song and shipped millions of board feet of hardwood lumber from the Smokies, but business being business, most insisted on driving a hard bargain for their cut-over property. The cost of creating Great Smoky Mountains National Park kept rising, much faster than private donations and state grants to buy the land were coming in.

Around 1927/28, the effort to preserve the Smokies reached its darkest hour. The campaign was $5 million short of what it needed to purchase the land, a seemingly insurmountable sum at the time, especially in southern Appalachia. School children had given pennies and dimes, boosters in Knoxville and Asheville had emptied their bank accounts, and the federal government felt obliged to stay out of the politically treacherous land acquisition business.

Leaders within the fledgling National Park Service turned to a very loyal and very rich friend, John D. Rockefeller, Jr., son of the oil tycoon. Mr. Rockefeller spent a lot of time in the out-of-doors, in national parks, and had a special affection for trees and old-growth forest. When he was informed of the situation in the Smokies, he pledged $5 million to the cause.

So momentous was the announcement of the Rockefeller gift that park proponents rang church bells and blew whistles throughout the city of Knoxville. Optimistic (overly, as it turned out) newspaper editors and civic leaders boasted that property values in the city would soon double, thanks to tourism. Mrs. Bridges's vision of a national park in her beloved Smokies was about to become real.

Although the cost of creating Great Smoky Mountains National Park was high, both in dollars and human misery, the end result is a sanctuary whose value is beyond measure. National park status rescued a place that was rapidly on its way to becoming another sad, worn-out piece of Appalachia. By the time the park was established, deer had nearly vanished from region. Bear were few and far between. The river otter was gone and its streams were too warm and choked with silt for native brook trout to survive. More than 75 percent of the grandest hardwood forest in eastern North America was clearcut and its residual slash burned in catastrophic fires. Wilderness had been beaten back to the highest peaks and steepest slopes of the Smokies.

Park protection has been so successful that today more than 1,500 black bears roam the 800 square mile preserve, a density of close to two bears per square mile. Smoky Mountain black bears are smaller than most black bears elsewhere; males average 250 pounds, females a mere 110. Despite their impressive strength and quickness (bears sprint at race horse speeds), black bears are mostly vegetarian. Summer berries and fall acorns are their staffs of life. When these aren't available, they get by on grasses, buds, roots, ants, grubs, and wasp larvae. Not that they won't grab a deer or chipmunk when they can, but most mammals, when in their prime and healthy, are always a step or two beyond a bear's reach.

Like any place with 1,500 bears and nine million human visitors a year, the Great Smoky Mountains have seen their share of conflicts between wildlife and people. Most problems start with food. For a big animal who usually earns his living tearing open yellowjacket nests or climbing the spindly branches of a cherry tree, the sight of five pounds of chicken on a picnic table must resemble the Holy Grail. So great is the temptation of our fat-laden fare that it takes only a couple of successful grabs before he mostly forsakes wild food and begins concentrating the whole of his efforts on picnic tables and garbage dumpsters.

Though the picnic basket–grabbing black bear is not without its comic side, the long-term effect is pathetic and tragic. A couple years back, a Smokies dumpster bear was actually hoisted into the back of a garbage truck where it was jostled and compacted for hours before being disgorged, with serious internal injuries, into the county landfill. More typically, however, the bear becomes ever more accustomed to the presence of people as it roams their environs. It learns that charging people usually causes them to abandon their food. The distinction between where the hot dog ends and the outstretched hand begins gets blurry. The reality of a big, powerful predator sharing space with vacationing families suddenly hits home.

Though multitudes of bear bites, lacerations, scratches and other relatively minor injuries have been suffered in the Smokies, there is only one bear-caused human fatality in the park's long history. That incident involved a lone woman sitting beside a river in the park's backcountry and an undersized female black bear and her yearling cub. Because there were no witnesses, the complete circumstances of the event are unknown, but evidence indicates that the bears ultimately acted in a predatory fashion.

Diligence by park rangers keeps most bear–human conflicts from developing in the first place. Though some of the old darting and tranquilizing still goes on, the real battles are now waged in the trash cans and campground fire pits. Keeping picnic areas and camp spots meticulously free of food scraps prevents the timid, truly wild bear from ever venturing beyond the trees in the first place.

The successful preservation of the Great Smoky Mountains is allowing some past wrongs to be righted. In 2001, the Park Service began an experimental program to reintroduce elk to the Smokies. Elk are native to the southern Appalachians and most of the East but were wiped out by unregulated hunting and changes in land use more than 150 years ago. So far the experiment seems to be working. In the autumn, park visitors can now watch majestically antlered males strut across golden meadows and challenge other bulls to sparring matches. Their long, eerie bugling echos up and down the valleys, a courting call to females and warning to rivals. During summer, cows give birth to spindly legged calves, who, in only a few days, are up and galloping through the woods.

Other homecomings have also been successful. River otters, peregrine falcons, and four species of threatened fish have all been reintroduced to the park. The ark of life that is the Great Smoky Mountains is being replenished, this time thanks to the actions of humankind.

As cities and suburbs continue to sprawl, the value of sanctuaries like Great Smoky Mountains National Park rises exponentially.

Years of research has revealed that, for certain species of migratory songbirds, it takes a large area of untrammeled forest like the Smokies to maintain a population. The Smokies are one of the few places in the East where species like the wood thrush can increase their populations enough to help replenish outside areas where forest fragmentation has forced a decline.

Economically valuable plants that are becoming scarce in the East—like ginseng, ramps, black cohosh, galax, orchids, and trilliums—still find refuge in the great garden of the Smoky Mountains. So rare and precious is the park's 50,000–100,000 acres of old-growth forest that it is one of the few places where scientists can study what life was like throughout the East only 250 years ago.

The founding families of this region, the Caldwells, Ogles, Woodys, Maples, Olivers, McCarters, and all the rest, can no longer live in the Great Smoky Mountains, but many still live as close as they can. They can lead you up a shady, overgrown path to the crumbling chimney that marks the site of their great grandparents' farm and tell you stories of old-time mountain life, what an Eden of plump wild berries and streams filled with trout it all was. They'll be sure to tell you their roots run deep in the Great Smoky Mountains, the most beautiful mountains in the world, and that though they can no longer live here, they can come home whenever, and just as often, as they wish.

Coneflower brightens the high-elevation spruce-fir forest in late summer.

ABOVE: Almost apelike at times, Smoky Mountain black bears spend much of their lives in trees.
PHOTO BY BILL LEA.

LEFT: West Prong, Little Pigeon River, named for the passenger pigeons that once darkened the skies above.

ABOVE: Rare maroon trilliums have a foul smell that attracts pollinating insects with a taste for carrion.

ABOVE: Beaked violet grows in rich forests and hemlock woods during April and May.

FACING PAGE: Towering Mingo Falls is on the Cherokee Indian Reservation, just outside the boundary of Great Smoky Mountains National Park.

ABOVE: Isolated Cataloochee Valley is a favorite place for hikers, anglers, and equestrians.
PHOTO BY BILL LEA.

FACING PAGE: Noah "Bud" Ogle's sturdy log home sits in the highlands above Gatlinburg along Cherokee Orchard Road. Many residents of Sevier County in East Tennessee can trace their lineage to this ruggedly beautiful mountain farm.

ABOVE: Catawba rhododendron blooms along the Blue Ridge Parkway, a 469-mile scenic road that connects the Smokies and Shenandoah National Park.

FACING PAGE: Eastern bluebirds nest in tree cavities and fence posts and are permanent residents in the Great Smoky Mountains.

ABOVE: Visitors to Cades Cove can usually count on seeing dozens of white-tailed deer in the open fields and along the forest edges.

LEFT: Flowering dogwood blooms bring the mountains to life in mid-April.

FOLLOWING PAGES: A magical sunrise reveals ridge after ridge stretching as far as the eye can see.

17

ABOVE: Pine needles and maple leaves weave a brightly colored tapestry on the forest floor.

LEFT: The Oconaluftee River is strewn with truck-sized boulders that mountain folk called "graybacks."

ABOVE: Late snow dusts a maple tree.

RIGHT: Morning light illuminates snow-covered Roundtop Mountain and the piney ridges beyond.

ABOVE: A male northern cardinal strikes a picturesque pose in a hawthorn tree.

LEFT: During winter, rainbow trout and other aquatic life slow down but are still active in the West Prong of the Little Pigeon River.

ABOVE: Flame azalea is a spectacular southern Appalachian shrub with bold flowers that range in color from cream to vibrant red.

LEFT: Rain-swollen Le Conte Creek rushes from its mile-high headwaters toward the town of Gatlinburg.

ABOVE: The Great Smoky Mountains host some of the richest, most diverse temperate hardwood forests on Earth. In October the beauty of the fall foliage is astonishing.

FACING PAGE: This Methodist church has stood in Cades Cove since 1902. It is just one of the many interesting stops along the 11-mile Cades Cove Loop Road.

ABOVE: A maple leaf floats downstream in a cool autumn brook.

ABOVE RIGHT: The "chick-a-dee-dee-dee" and "fee-be-fee-bu" songs of the Carolina chickadee are familiar sounds of the Great Smoky Mountain forest.

FACING PAGE: The icy water that feeds Rainbow Falls plummets from the rocky slopes of Mt. Le Conte.

LEFT: Despite its name, Little River is one of the larger streams in the Smokies. It is also one of the park's most productive trout streams.

BELOW: Fishing spiders grow as large as the palm of your hand and will definitely startle you if you happen upon one. Some species of fishing spiders actually do fish, running across the surface of the water to grab tadpoles and minnows.

FOLLOWING PAGES: At the higher elevations of the Great Smoky Mountains, fall colors often reach their peak in early October. This view is from the Newfound Gap Road looking toward the Deep Creek Valley.

RIGHT: Roaring Fork descends toward Gatlinburg among moss-covered boulders and over-hanging rosebay rhododendron.

BELOW: As its name implies, the diminutive Cope's gray treefrog spends most of its time hidden among the branches of shrubs and trees. Some mountain folk call it the "rain toad" because it may sing on rainy days in summer and fall.

ABOVE: A red-tailed hawk watches for mice, chipmunks, rabbits, and other potential prey.

LEFT: Sunset at Clingmans Dome. At 6,643 feet, Clingmans is the highest mountain in the Smokies and the third highest east of the Mississippi.

ABOVE: The Cable Mill historic area is located halfway around the Cades Cove Loop Road.
The site features a preserved home, barn, blacksmith shop, water-powered grist mill, and the
sorghum mill shown here in the foreground.

FACING PAGE: Before establishment of the national park, farmers grew hay, wheat, corn, oats, and rye
in Cades Cove. Today the scenic valley is preserved for the benefit of wildlife and the visiting public.

ABOVE: During wet years, well over 7 feet of rain and snow drench the Smoky Mountain high country. All this precipitation feeds more than 2,000 miles of streams in the park.

FACING PAGE: A high-elevation heath bald dominated by Catawba rhododendron bursts into bloom.

Snow may fall any time from late
October through mid-April in
the Great Smoky Mountains.

ABOVE: Pileated woodpeckers are one of the most frequently seen birds in the Smokies. They stand 16 inches tall and sport a bright red crest that makes them hard to miss. PHOTO BY BILL LEA.

RIGHT: Sumac shrubs provide some of the earliest and brightest fall colors.

ABOVE: With a wingspan of more than 4 inches, the spectacular luna moth is one of the largest moths in North America. The spots on the backs of its wings may look like eyes to birds and other potential predators.

LEFT: A short hike out of Deep Creek Campground will take you to pretty Indian Creek Falls.

ABOVE: An eastern bluebird holds breakfast in his beak while conveniently posing beside a blooming day lily.

RIGHT: Mt. Cammerer reaches nearly 5,000 feet. A historic stone fire tower sits atop its rocky summit.

ABOVE: Black bear cub is amused by fallen tree limbs.

RIGHT: Footprints of a black bear.

FACING PAGE: In the Smokies, spring greens start in the valleys in April and gradually climb the slopes. Trees at the highest elevations aren't completely leafed out until late May or early June.

ABOVE: An elegant maidenhair fern.

FACING PAGE: The remote Big Creek area is a favorite among hikers and equestrians in the know.

ABOVE: Red fox siblings stand near the entrance to their den.

FACING PAGE: A massive tuliptree towers above a hiker.
Tuliptrees grow remarkably straight and shed their lower
branches as they mature.

ABOVE: Anglers ply the cold, clear waters of the Little Pigeon River for trout.

RIGHT: Bluejays can be found year-round in the Smokies.

FACING PAGE: The Old Mill in Pigeon Forge uses the waters of the West Prong of the Little Pigeon River for power.

ABOVE: The wild turkey has made an amazing comeback in the Great Smoky Mountains. Flocks of the 3-foot-tall birds are now frequently seen in open woods and fields throughout the national park.

LEFT: Sassafras and sumac flourish in an old farm field in the Oconaluftee River Valley.

FOLLOWING PAGES: Dawn from Clingmans Dome. The Great Smoky Mountains were named for the swirling clouds, rising streamers of mist, and persistent smokelike haze that is so often present.

LEFT: Mouse Creek joins Big Creek in a frothy cascade.

BELOW: New York ferns blanket the forest floor.

ABOVE: A family of bicyclists uses a backroad to cut across the center of Cades Cove.

LEFT: A solitary black walnut tree casts a long afternoon shadow in Cades Cove.

RIGHT: Flowering dogwoods are understory trees that spread their branches wide to absorb the diminished sunlight filtered by taller overstory trees.

BELOW: Eastern cottontail rabbits like this one must constantly be on the lookout for bobcats, foxes, coyotes, hawks, and other predators.

ABOVE LEFT: Children play the Cherokee game of stick ball.

ABOVE RIGHT: Suzanna George demonstrates the Cherokee's unique style of pottery making.

LEFT: Velma Lossiah uses beads to create beautiful belts and jewelry.

FACING PAGE: The Mountain Farm Museum preserves historic buildings as well as heirloom varieties of garden vegetables, fruit trees, and row crops.

ABOVE: Approximately 70 of the Appalachian Trail's 2,100 miles run through Great Smoky Mountains National Park.

RIGHT: Great Smoky Mountains National Park is a preserve for creatures great and small, including this tiny jumping spider.

FACING PAGE: White trilliums announce that spring has truly arrived.

ABOVE: This scarlet tanager will leave the Smokies in October for wintering grounds in South America. In contrast, the much less cosmopolitan red-cheeked Jordan's salamander can be found only within the boundaries of Great Smoky Mountains National Park.

LEFT: Nearly 100 species of native trees grow in the Great Smoky Mountains. This variety makes for a rich and interesting tapestry of color each autumn.

ABOVE: The blooms of rosebay rhododendron adorn the steep slopes and streamsides of the Smokies throughout the summer.

LEFT: Sunset from Morton Overlook on Newfound Gap Road.

ABOVE: Colorful autumn leaves first decorate the trees, then, for a fading few days, the streams and forest floor.

LEFT: The polyphemus moth has a wingspan of more than 5 inches and is common in the hardwood forests of the East. Like other moths, it feeds voraciously as a caterpillar but not at all as an adult.

FACING PAGE: Cataloochee Creek courses through the broad and historic Cataloochee Valley. PHOTO BY BILL LEA.

ABOVE: Blooming from late October into January, the small witch hazel tree is the first and last plant to flower in the Smokies each year. An extract made from the tree has been used to soothe bruises, burns, and sore muscles for centuries.

LEFT: The substantial waters of Little River tumble toward a thundering waterfall called The Sinks.

LEFT (TOP TO BOTTOM): Mountain spiderwort lives in dry woods at the low and middle elevations.

Women once used the fragrant flowers of sweetshrub as perfume.

Spring beauty is one of the most common and delightful wildflowers in the Smokies.

FACING PAGE: Bluebead lily blooms among ferns in the Smoky Mountain high country.

ABOVE: White-tailed bucks size each other up.

LEFT: Early morning fog brings enchantment to the fields of Cades Cove.

ABOVE: Red spruce trees along Newfound Gap Road with a dusting of snow. The climate at the park's higher elevations is similar to southeastern Canada's.

LEFT: Gray squirrels prepare for winter by caching acorns and other foods during autumn.

FACING PAGE: Cosby Creek freshly dressed in snow.

ABOVE: Early saxifrage is a northern plant that is near the southern limit of its range in the Smokies.

FACING PAGE: The rushing waters of Big Creek.

ABOVE: Squirrel corn blooms in rich woods from April into May.

ABOVE: The restored Great Smoky Mountain Railway offers train rides through the mountains of western North Carolina.

FACING PAGE: Fog makes the movement of air currents visible to the human eye. During certain weather conditions, clouds fill the valleys, then pour through gaps in the ridges.

ABOVE: A buckeye butterfly rests on a bull thistle.

FACING PAGE: Before the establishment of Great Smoky Mountains National Park, more than 700 people lived in Cades Cove.

ABOVE: Palm warblers pass through the Great Smoky Mountains on their way to and from wintering grounds in the southern United States and Mexico.

LEFT: Mid-summer in the Smokies: purple-fringed orchid blooms amid ferns.

ABOVE: A late autumn near the Oconaluftee Valley Visitor Center.

FACING PAGE: Horses from the Cades Cove riding stables occasionally earn the privilege to graze the cove's lush meadows.

FACING PAGE: Autumn view of Deep Creek Valley from Newfound Gap Road.

BELOW: Little River is fed by myriad springs as it pours from steep slopes near the Appalachian Trail toward Elkmont and Townsend.

ABOVE: Autumn leaves and pine cones.

RIGHT: Beautiful rose-breasted grosbeaks are occasionally glimpsed in the northern hardwood forests of the Smokies during the summer breeding season.

FACING PAGE: August in the Smoky Mountain high country: bee balm, white snakeroot, and angelica.

ABOVE: Fringed phacelia and mayapple carpet the floor of a cove hardwood forest.

FACING PAGE: Abundant water is the lifeblood of the 100,000 species of plants and animals that scientists estimate live within Great Smoky Mountains National Park.

LEFT: Raccoons harvest crayfish, frogs, and fish from Smoky Mountain streams. PHOTO BY BILL LEA.

BELOW: Though seldom seen, bobcats are quite common. They hunt squirrels, mice, birds, and even box turtles.

FACING PAGE: Flowering dogwood trees typically turn crimson in September.

ABOVE: The eastern screech owl's large eyes afford it the vision to swoop through the deep forest at night.

LEFT: Sixteen peaks in the Great Smoky Mountains reach above 6,000 feet.

RIGHT: Snow-covered red spruce trees at Newfound Gap.

BELOW: The dark-eyed junco usually spends summers in the spruce-fir forest and winters in the lowlands.

ABOVE: American goldfinches are often found near thistles.

FACING PAGE: Red maple, yellow birch, American beech,
and other hardwoods light up Thomas Ridge in autumn.

ABOVE: A kayaker risks the rocky waters of the Little Pigeon.

LEFT: Boulders slewed from high in the Smokies fill streams like the Little Pigeon River in Greenbrier.

ABOVE: The Tipton place in Cades Cove is one of more than 100 historic structures preserved by the National Park Service.

FACING PAGE: Oak trees like this one attract bears when acorns appear in late summer.

ABOVE: During their terrestrial eft stage, red-spotted newts wander far from water.
PHOTO BY BILL LEA.

FACING PAGE: Moss-covered rocks like these usually indicate that the stream
is not prone to catastrophic flash floods.

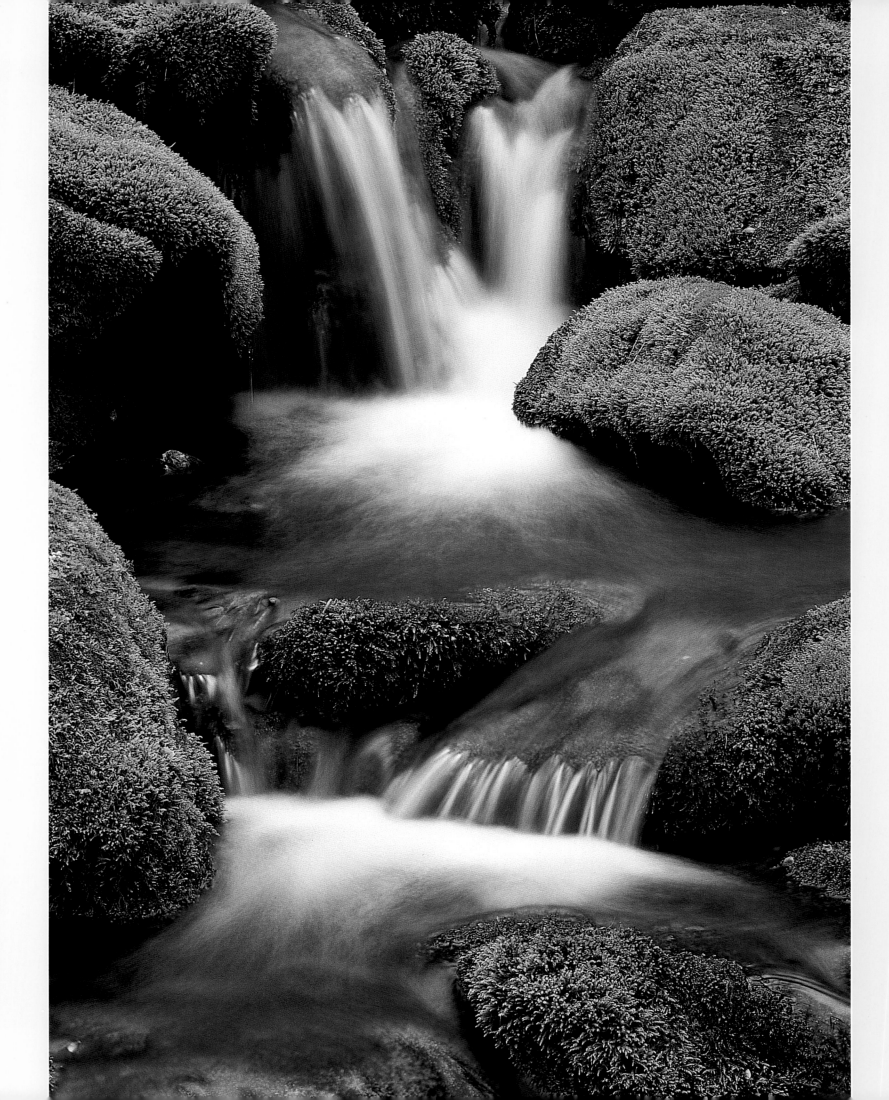

LEFT: A summer thunderstorm arrives in the Great Smoky Mountains.

FOLLOWING PAGE: The rose-colored flowers of Catawba rhododendron are always a delight to behold.